C is for Christ

Author: Dr. C. White-Elliott
Illustrated by: Marina Prince

www.clfpublishing.org
909.315.3161

Copyright © 2020 by Cassundra White-Elliott

All rights reserved. No portion of this book may be reproduced, stored in a retrieval system, or transmitted by any form or any means electronically, photocopied, recorded, or any other except for brief quotations in printed reviews, without the prior permission of the publisher.

Illustrations by Marina Prince.

Contact Info: marina.olivia.prince@gmail.com

ISBN # 978-1-945102-46-2

Printed in the United States of America.

For Aaron M. White II

my grandson

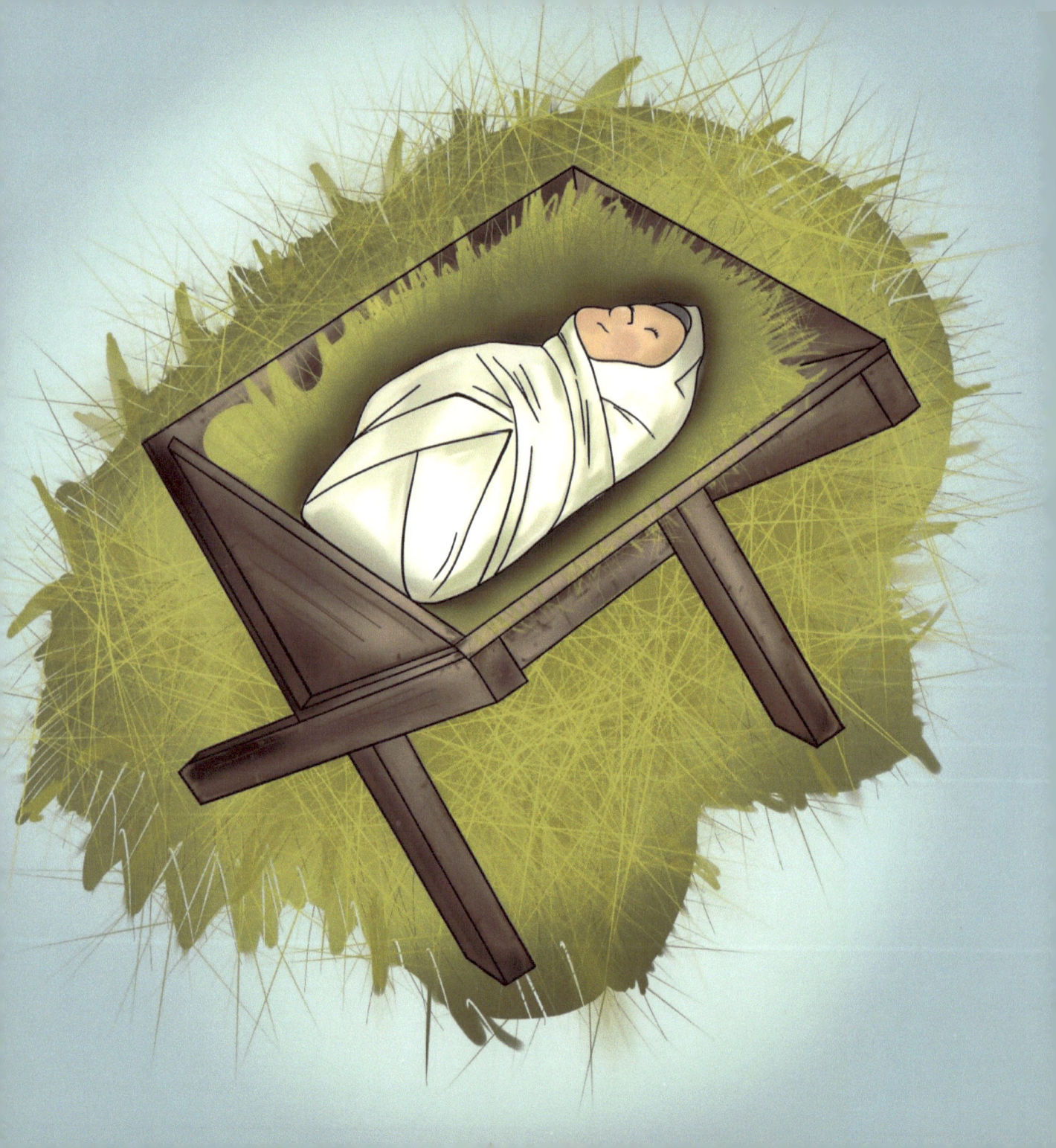

At the time Jesus was born, his mother Mary and his earthly father Joseph were traveling. They tried to get a room at an inn, so Mary could be comfortable. But, the inn had no empty rooms. When the time came for Mary to give birth, she had no other choice but to go into the stable where the animals were kept. When Jesus was born, he was placed in a manger and wrapped in a cloth.

When Jesus was around twelve years old, he traveled with his parents to a festival. After the festival was over, his parents began making the trip back home. They lost sight of Jesus, thinking he was somewhere in the group of family. They began to ask around, so they could find their son. It took three days to find him. Little did they know, Jesus was in the temple, and he was listening to the men speak, and he was asking them questions.

Later, when Jesus was thirty years old, he began to do the job he came to earth for. Before he could begin, he wanted to be baptized. So, he went to John the Baptist. After John baptized Jesus, a dove flew down from heaven, and a loud voice was heard from heaven. It was the voice of God saying, "This is my Son, whom I love; with him I am well pleased."

After Jesus was baptized, he went into the wilderness, to spend some time alone with God, his father. He prayed for forty days and nights. While he was there, he did not eat. So, he became weak. Then, the devil began to talk to him. The devil made promises to Jesus to get him to go along with his plan. But, Jesus wanted to do what his father desired instead. So, he did not give in to the devil.

Jesus chose twelve men to travel with him to share the good news about God. The men were named Simon Peter, Andrew, James (the son of Zebedee), John, Philip, Bartholomew, Thomas, Matthew, James (the son of Alphaeus), Thaddaeus, Simon the Zealot, and Judas Iscariot. They traveled with Jesus every where he went.

After Jesus spread the good news of God for three and a half years, some mean men wanted to kill him. They accused him of saying bad things. The men hung Jesus on a cross. On the cross, Jesus died. The men did not understand that Jesus already knew he would die on a cross. That is why Jesus was born. He came to give his life for every person. Jesus gave his life, so we could reconnect with God.

After Jesus died on the cross, he was buried later that day. But, three days later, no one could find Jesus' body in the grave. He had come back to life!
Then, after living on earth for another forty days, Jesus went back to heaven to be with God, his father.

Remember, Jesus is still alive today.
He lives in heaven, and he lives in our hearts.

www.ingramcontent.com/pod-product-compliance
Lightning Source LLC
Chambersburg PA
CBHW040121170426
42813CB00110B/2900